Veggie Bites

A LITTLE BOOK OF TEMPTING VEGETARIAN RECIPES

Published in association with

RAVENSWOOD
Caring about people with learning disabilities

GRUB STREET · LONDON

Acknowledgements

This book was compiled entirely through voluntary contribution and effort. Ravenswood would like to thank all the volunteers involved and especially the following:

Recipes written by: Paul Osborne
(Catering Manager at The Deli)

. . .

Recipes chosen by: Trainees at The Deli

. . .

Production Team:
Shaun Askew, Gidon Cohen, Rachel Finestein
(Production, design, layout and typographical arrangement)
Illustrator/Cartoonist: Shaun Askew
Cover illustration: John Valley

. . .

Additional thanks to: Harvey Zalud, Johnny Gould, Susie Faux, Jonathan Cowan, Linzi Pinto, David Finestein, Julia Hollenberry, Jo-Anne Parker, Elaine Cohen, Lawrence Glyn, Anne Finestein, Computers Unlimited, Laura de Friend
Some of the many employers who have shown their support for the project by recruiting The Deli trainees are:
Asda · Barnet Corporation · Coppets Wood Hospital
Forte (Trusthouse Forte) · Guardian Royal Exchange
Hill Samuel · John Lewis · McDonalds · Middlesex Polytechnic
Owen & Owen · St. Theresa's School · Sobell Day Centre

Published by Grub Street
The Basement, 10 Chivalry Road, London SW11 1HT

Copyright © Grub Street 1993
Text, illustrations and design © 1993
Ravenswood Foundation and Askew, Cohen and Finestein

British Library Cataloguing in Publication Data
Veggie Bites
641.5
ISBN 0-948817-81-X

Printed and bound in Slovenia by Gorenjski tisk.

CONTENTS......

About
Ravenswood

By purchasing a copy of *Veggie Bites*, you are helping young people with learning disabilities to be successful in the competitive world of work.

All proceeds from the sale of this book go to Ravenswood's government-approved Youth Training scheme, The Deli, one of very few specifically designed for people aged from 16 to 25 years with learning disabilities.

The Deli follows an Equal Opportunities policy, and is open to all young people, irrespective of ethnic background or religion. What matters is that they need training, and help in finding employment. Ravenswood gives that help.

Ravenswood is a major independent charity working for people with learning disabilities. The Deli is part of its network of caring services, which includes residential, day and respite care, education, training, recreation and social services.

Although a learning disability is a permanent condition, progress can still be made. Ravenswood believes that every child is educable, that young people benefit from training and that older people, who may have spent a lifetime in long-stay hospitals, can be successfully resettled into the community.

The Deli, which operates at three London locations, places major emphasis on encouraging trainees to find a niche in the world of work. The employment department tries to ensure that suitable work experience placements are found, as well as suitable jobs upon successful completion of the programme. We are pleased to say that the scheme has had a high rate of success in placing young people in full or part-time employment.

The Deli's After Care Officer ensures that the trainees are not alone during their initial introduction to working life. Individual support from Ravenswood is available for a full year.

Deli trainees have chosen the recipes in this book, and they hope that you will enjoy their *Veggie Bites*.

Thank you for your support.

Ravenswood
17 Highfield Road
London
NW11 9DZ

FOREWORD

In this, Ravenswood's 40th birthday year, I am delighted to help, in a small way, with the celebration edition of *Veggie Bites* to assist The Deli, a Youth Training scheme for young people with learning difficulties.
To help entice you into the kitchen, here is a selection of forty delicious recipes - one for each year that this caring charity has been in existence helping families to cope with everyday life, something that too many of us take for granted.

Food is a universal bond, so many of us feel passionately about it and, of course, it cuts across all barriers. For me, it has been a passport to the world, enabling me to travel and experience new adventures.
Healthy food does not mean a life of deprivation. On the contrary, I want to celebrate the delights and pleasures of eating food that is light and wholesome and looks irresistible. After all, we all have to eat to maintain life, so why not make it an experience that you can look forward to? Healthy eating should become everyone's priority.

Cooking and eating should be interesting, exciting, different and, above all, fun. The ingredients for courses should differ in content for both interest and nutritional balance. Colour, too, is a vital ingredient of menu planning. The colours of food in a meal should be considered as carefully as the balance. Tastes, too, are obviously vital to the success of a dish or a meal: an imaginative cook is continually experimenting, marrying flavours, to create something new and different. Try to include and mix the flavours of sweet, salt, sour and bitter to achieve a good flavour balance.

Finally, perhaps one of the most important things to remember about menu planning is not to plan too meticulously! The good, creative cook should never have set ideas when shopping for the basic ingredients, but should buy what is best, what is good that day. The essential ingredient, is, in effect, flexibility.
Happy cooking to you all.

Anton Mosimann

Soups

CREAM OF
m u s h r o o m   s o u p

2oz (60g)	Butter
2oz (60g)	Onion, sliced
2oz (60g)	Leek, sliced
2oz (60g)	Celery
2pts (1¼ltr)	Vegetable stock
2oz (60g)	Plain flour
4oz (120g)	White mushrooms, chopped
¼pt (150 ml)	Single cream
	Bouquet garni
	Salt and pepper

METHOD

1. Gently cook the sliced onions, leeks and celery in the butter without letting them brown.
2. Mix in the flour and cook over a gentle heat while still making sure no browning occurs.
3. Gradually mix in the vegetable stock.
4. Stir to the boil, add the washed and chopped mushrooms, bouquet garni and season.
5. Simmer for 30 - 45 minutes.
6. Remove bouquet garni.
7. Pass the pan contents through a sieve.
8. Return liquid to a clean saucepan.
9. Reheat the soup and add the cream before serving.

CREAM OF
m u s t a r d   s o u p

1oz (30g)	Butter
1 bunch	Spring onions, chopped
1 tbl	Mustard powder
1 tbl	Flour
2 tbls	Dijon mustard
½ tbl	Lemon juice
2	Egg yolks
½pt (300ml)	Single cream
1pt (600ml)	Vegetable stock
	Salt and pepper

METHOD

1. Melt butter in saucepan and add spring onions. Cook for 5 minutes.
2. Stir in mustard powder and flour. Cook for a minute.
3. Stir in stock, Dijon mustard and lemon juice. Simmer for 5 minutes.
4. Beat together egg yolks, cream and seasoning.
5. Stir into soup and cook over a gentle heat, being careful not to boil.
6. Garnish with chopped spring onions and serve hot with cheese scones (see page 26).

CARROT
& Coriander soup

2oz (60g)	Butter
1lb (480g)	Carrots, sliced
2oz (60g)	Onion, sliced
2oz (60g)	Leek, sliced
2oz (60g)	Celery, sliced
1oz (30g)	Plain flour
½ tsp	Tomato puree
2pt (1¼ltr)	Vegetable stock
1 bunch	Fresh coriander
	Bouquet garni
	Salt and pepper

METHOD

1. Gently cook all the sliced vegetables in the butter until soft, without browning and then mix in the flour.
2. Mix in the tomato puree.
3. Gradually add the vegetable stock.
4. Bring to boil whilst stirring, then add the coriander, retaining a few leaves for garnish, bouquet garni and seasoning.
5. Simmer for about 50 minutes.
6. Remove bouquet garni.
7. Pass contents of pan through a sieve and return liquid to pan.
8. Reheat and serve with a fresh leaf of coriander.
9. Croutons may also be served.

L ENTIL
s o u p

INGREDIENTS

8oz (240g)	Lentils
2pts (1¼ltr)	Vegetable stock
2oz (60g)	Onion, chopped
2oz (60g)	Carrot, chopped
1 tsp	Tomato puree
	Bouquet garni
	Salt and pepper

METHOD

1. Wash and pick out the bad or discoloured lentils.
2. Place lentils in a saucepan and cover with vegetable stock.
3. Bring to the boil and add the bouquet garni.
4. Add all the remaining ingredients to the pan and season.
5. Simmer until tender, skimming the surface as necessary.
6. Remove bouquet garni.
7. Pass through sieve.
8. Reheat soup. Serve with croutons.

FRENCH
onion soup

2lb (1kg)	Onions
1oz (30g)	Butter
½ oz (15g)	Plain flour
3pts (1¼ ltr)	Vegetable stock
	Salt and pepper

1. Peel the onions, halve and slice.
2. Melt the butter, add the onions and cook slowly until browned.
3. Mix in the flour and cook over a gentle heat until lightly brown.
4. Gradually mix in the stock, bring to the boil and season.
5. Simmer for 15 minutes.
6. Serve hot with toasted slices of French bread with grated cheese.

FARMHOUSE
vegetable soup

1 tbl	Oil
6oz (180g)	Leeks, chopped
6oz (180g)	Onion, chopped
6oz (180g)	Carrots, chopped
6oz (180g)	Potatoes, chopped
6oz (180g)	Celery, chopped
12oz (360g)	Can of peeled tomatoes
1¾ pts (1ltr)	Vegetable stock
7oz (200g)	Sweetcorn
8oz (240g)	Peas
8oz (240g)	Green beans
	Bouquet garni
¼ tsp	Thyme
¼ tsp	Basil

METHOD

1. Gently cook the chopped leeks and onion in the oil.
2. Add the chopped carrots, potatoes, celery, tomatoes and their juice.
3. Then stir in the stock, salt and pepper, basil, thyme and add bouquet garni.
4. Bring to the boil, reduce the heat and simmer for 30 minutes or until the vegetables are tender.
5. Remove bouquet garni.
6. Add the sweetcorn, beans and peas and cook for 5 - 10 minutes.
7. Serve with home-baked crusty bread.

WILD NETTLE
s o u p

8oz (240g)	Fresh young nettles, stinging nettles
2oz (60g)	Onions, sliced
2oz (60g)	Celery, sliced
2oz (60g)	Chives, sliced
2 cloves	Garlic, crushed
2oz (60g)	Butter
2oz (60g)	Plain flour
2pts (1¼ltr)	Vegetable stock
	Bouquet garni
	Seasoning

METHOD

1. Gently cook all the vegetables in the butter without colouring.
2. Stir in the flour and cook slowly for several minutes, again without colouring.
3. Gradually stir in the hot vegetable stock.
4. Bring to the boil, add the bouquet garni and seasoning.
5. Simmer for 45 minutes.
6. Remove the bouquet garni and pass through a sieve or liquidise.
7. Return to a clean saucepan, reboil and adjust the seasoning to your personal taste.

Please note: Use only young nettles picked well away from roadside pollution and weedkillers.

CREAM OF
tomato & rice soup

2oz (60g)	Butter
4oz (120g)	Onion, diced
4oz (120g)	Carrot, diced
2oz (60g)	Plain flour
2pts (1¼ ltr)	Vegetable stock
2oz (60g)	Tomato puree
1oz (30g)	Cooked rice
½pt (300ml)	Single cream
	Bouquet garni
	Salt and pepper

METHOD

1. Melt the butter in a pan.
2. Add the diced onion and carrot and lightly brown.
3. Mix in the flour and cook until the mixture has a sandy texture.
4. Remove from the heat, add the tomato puree.
5. Return to the heat and slowly add the vegetable stock.
6. Stir gently while bringing to the boil.
7. Add the bouquet garni, adjust the seasoning.
8. Simmer for about 1 hour.
9. Remove the bouquet garni.
10. Pass contents of pan through a sieve and return liquid to the pan.
11. Reheat the soup, add the cooked rice and cream.
12. Serve with croutons.

Pumpkin
s o u p

INGREDIENTS

2oz (60g)	Butter
1	Onion, chopped
2 lb (1kg)	Pumpkin
2oz (60g)	Plain flour
2 pts (1¼ ltr)	Vegetable stock
½ pt (300 ml)	Milk
	Salt and pepper to taste
	Pinch of nutmeg
1oz (30g)	Mixed herbs

METHOD

1. Melt butter, add chopped onion and pumpkin, allow to sweat for 10 minutes.
2. Add flour and stir.
3. Gradually add vegetable stock, nutmeg and herbs.
4. Bring to the boil then simmer until pumpkin is tender.
5. Season and sieve soup.
6. Blend in milk and garnish with fresh herbs and cream.
7. Serve hot with croutons.

Main courses

CHEESE SCONES

3oz (90g)	Plain wholewheat flour
3oz (90g)	Plain flour
1 tsp	Baking powder
¼ tsp	Mustard powder
1oz (30g)	Butter
3oz (90g)	Grated cheese
1	Egg
2-3 tbls	Milk

KENTISH
vegetable cobbler

INGREDIENTS	
1oz (30g)	Butter
1	Onion, chopped
2	Carrots, sliced
1	Courgette, sliced
2 stalks	Celery
4oz (120g)	Mushrooms, sliced
3	Tomatoes
15oz (450g)	Butter beans
	Seasoning

METHOD

1. Melt butter in saucepan, gently cook onion and carrots until soft, then stir in courgette, celery and mushrooms. Blend well.
2. Cover and cook for 5 minutes and stir in the tomatoes, beans and seasoning.
3. Now make the cheese scones as follows:-
   Mix together the flour with the baking powder, a pinch of salt and mustard powder. Rub in the butter until the mixture looks like fine breadcrumbs.
   Stir in the grated cheese.
   Bind together with a beaten egg and add enough milk to make a soft dough.
   Roll out dough and cut out into pieces ¾ inch (2cm) thick and 2¼ inch (6cm) round.
4. Spoon the vegetable mixture into an ovenproof dish, top with the scones, brush with a little milk.
5. Bake in a preheated oven (450 °F, 230° C, Gas mark 6) for about 20 minutes. Serve hot.

Homity
pie

PASTRY	
12oz (360g)	Plain flour
6oz (180g)	Butter or margarine
Pinch	Salt
3-5 tbls	Cold water

FILLING	
1 large	Onion, chopped
2 cloves	Garlic, chopped
8oz (240g)	Vegetarian cheese
3 tbls	Fresh parsley, chopped
¼ pt (150 ml)	Single cream
1½ lb (750g)	Cooked potatoes, sliced
	Seasoning

METHOD

1. Rub the fat into flour adding a little water if necessary to make pastry dough.
2. Line a 8inch (20 cm) pie dish with the dough.
3. Mix the chopped onion, garlic and parsley.
4. Place a layer of sliced potatoes in the pie dish.
5. Now add a layer of onion, garlic and parsley. Season well and add a layer of grated cheese.
6. Continue to layer ingredients as above until used up.
7. Pour the cream over the top evenly.
8. Cover with the remaining pastry and brush on egg wash.
8. Place in a moderate oven for approximately 45 minutes (350° F, 180° C, Gas mark 4).
9. Serve hot or cold.

MUSHROOM
c a r b o n a r a

1oz (30g)	Butter
1 tbl	Oil
1 clove	Garlic
1	Medium onion, chopped
6oz (180g)	Button mushrooms, sliced
3	Eggs
1½ pt (900ml)	Double cream
3oz (90g)	Parmesan cheese, grated
1lb (480g)	Spaghetti
	Salt and pepper

METHOD

1. Place a large ovenproof dish or bowl in a pre-heated oven.
2. Heat the oil and butter in a frying pan and add the garlic and chopped onion, cook until light golden in colour.
3. Add the sliced mushrooms, cook for a few minutes, then put aside and keep warm on a very low heat.
4. Beat eggs and the cream together, stir in the cheese, salt and pepper. Keep this to one side.
5. Cook the spaghetti in salted water until tender. Drain. Transfer to heated dish.
6. Immediately stir in onion and mushroom mixture, then add cream, egg and cheese.
7. Using two forks, toss together throughly, sprinkle with chopped parsley and serve immediately.

S P I C Y   T O M A T O   S A U C E

1oz (30g)	Butter
1	Onion
1 clove	Garlic
14oz (420g)	Can of peeled tomatoes
2 stalks	Celery
1	Bay leaf

M E T H O D

1. Melt butter in saucepan and gently cook sliced onion and garlic until soft.
2. Add the tomatoes, chopped celery and bay leaf.
3. Simmer gently for 10 minutes, then remove bay leaf.
4. Liquidise the sauce until smooth.
5. Serve hot, garnished with chopped parsley.

CASHEW
n u t   l o a f

INGREDIENTS

1 tbl	Oil
1	Onion
2 cloves	Garlic
8oz (240g)	Cashew nuts
4oz (120g)	Fresh breadcrumbs
1	Egg
3	Cooked parsnips, mashed
1 tsp	Fresh rosemary and thyme
1 tsp	Yeast extract
¼pt (150ml)	Hot water
1oz (30g)	Butter
8oz (240g)	Mushrooms

METHOD

1. Heat oil, fry the onion and garlic until soft.
2. Grind the cashew nuts in a blender, then mix with the fresh breadcrumbs.
3. Beat in the egg and then add the parsnips, chopped herbs and fried onion along with its juices.
4. Dissolve the yeast extract in the hot water and add to the other ingredients. Season well.
5. Melt the butter in a frying pan and quickly fry the sliced mushrooms.
6. Grease a 2lb loaf tin with butter. Pour in half the nut mixture.
7. Place the fried mushrooms onto the mixture then top with remaining mixture.
8. Cover with tin foil and bake (350° F, 180° C, Gas mark 4) for 1 hour. Remove from the oven, leave for 20 minutes before turning out.
9. Serve hot or cold with spicy tomato sauce.

That Ovenproof dish is just SO shallow

CHEESE SAUCE

2oz (60g)	Plain flour
2oz (60g)	Butter
1pt (600ml)	Warm milk
2oz (60g)	Grated cheese

METHOD

1. Melt butter and add the flour while stirring all the time, and cook until the mixture has a sandy texture.
2. Gradually add the warm milk, stirring all the time.
3. Finally stir in the grated cheese.

VEGETARIAN
l a s a g n e

1 tbl	Oil
2	Onions
2	Red peppers
2	Green peppers
15oz (450g)	Can of peeled tomatoes
1 clove	Garlic
6oz (180g)	Tomato puree
1 tsp	Fresh mixed herbs
2oz (60g)	Grated cheese
6oz (180g)	Wholewheat lasagne
	Salt and pepper

METHOD

1. Heat oil in saucepan. Add the sliced onions and peppers and gently cook until soft.
2. Stir in the tomatoes, garlic, tomato puree, chopped herbs and seasoning, blend in well.
3. Simmer for about 30 minutes until thickened.
4. Prepare lasagne according to packet instructions.
5. Line a shallow ovenproof dish with lasagne.
6. Cover with a little of the tomato mixture. Top with another layer of pasta. Repeat the layers in this way until the pasta and tomato mixture is used. Finish with a layer of pasta.
7. Cover the top of the lasagne with the cheese sauce. Sprinkle the top with remaining cheese.
8. Bake in a preheated oven for 45 minutes (350° F, 180° C, Gas mark 4). Serve hot.

Risotto
Milanese

2oz (60g)	Butter
1	Onion, chopped
3oz (90g)	Mushrooms, sliced
1 clove	Garlic, crushed
8oz (240g)	Italian grain rice
1 pinch	Saffron powder
	Salt and pepper
1pt (600 ml)	Vegetable stock
¼ pt (150 ml)	White wine
3 tbls	Parmesan cheese

METHOD

1. Gently fry the onion, mushrooms and garlic in half the butter for about 5 minutes.
2. Add the rice and continue to fry for a further 5 minutes.
3. Add the saffron and half the stock, stirring until well mixed.
5. Add the white wine and stir.
6. Place the remaining butter over the top and sprinkle with the Parmesan cheese.
7. Cover the risotto until ready and stir once or twice with a fork.
8. Turn the risotto into a hot serving dish.
9. Serve with a fresh green salad.

BLACK-EYED
Pete's Casserole

9oz (270g)	Black-eyed beans
15oz (450g)	Can of plum tomatoes
1	Red onion, chopped
1 clove	Garlic, crushed
3oz (90g)	Tomato puree
½	Green pepper, diced
1pt (600ml)	Water
1	Vegetable stock cube
1oz (30g)	Fresh parsley, chopped
1oz (30g)	Fresh basil, chopped
1lb (480g)	Button mushrooms, sliced
10oz (300g)	Can of sweetcorn

METHOD

1. Cover the black-eyed beans with cold water and allow to soak overnight.
2. Drain the beans and place in a saucepan with sufficient water to cover, bring to boil and simmer for 30 minutes, then drain.
3. In a large saucepan mix the beans, tomatoes, onion, garlic,tomato puree, chopped pepper and the water. Add the vegetable stock cube.
4. Bring the saucepan to the boil, reduce the heat and simmer for 1 hour, stirring occasionally.
5. Add the parsley, basil, sliced mushrooms and sweetcorn. Mix well and simmer for a further 15 minutes.
6. Serve with hot crusty bread.

Spinach
& almond pancakes

PANCAKES	
2½ oz (75g)	Plain flour
2	Eggs
2 tsps	Oil
8 fl oz (220ml)	Milk
9oz (270g)	Spinach, cooked and chopped

FILLING	
2oz (60g)	Flaked almonds
9oz (270g)	Ricotta cheese
1 tbl	Breadcrumbs
1	Egg

METHOD

1. Sift the plain flour, add the eggs and oil.
2. Gradually stir in the milk.
3. Add the drained and chopped spinach to the batter.
4. Heat an oiled frying pan, pour in sufficient batter to coat the pan.
5. Cook slowly until brown, turn the pancake and brown the other side.
6. Turn out onto a plate. Cook the remaining ingredients.
7. To make the filling, combine the remaining ingredients.
8. Fill each pancake with the filling and place in an oven-proof dish.
9. Cook for approximately 10 minutes in a moderate oven (350° F, 180° C, Gas mark 4).
10. Serve with a tomato sauce.

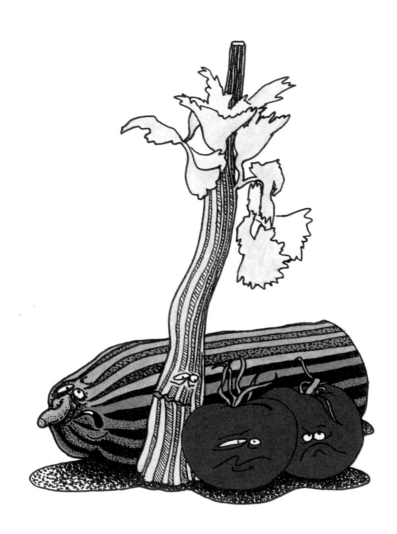

Salads

Mushrooms
a la grecque

INGREDIENTS

8oz (240g)	Button mushrooms
2½fl oz (75ml)	Olive oil
½ pt (300ml)	Water
1	Bay leaf
2 slices	Lemon
Pinch	Caraway seeds
	Salt

METHOD

1. Wash the mushrooms well and place in a saucepan with all the other ingredients.
2. Simmer for 15 - 20 minutes.
3. Serve cold in the liquor.

Cucumber
& dill salad

INGREDIENTS

1	Cucumber, diced
	Fresh dill, chopped
5oz (150g)	Natural yoghurt

METHOD

1. Mix all ingredients together and chill before serving.

DELI
rice salad

4oz (120g)	Cooked brown rice
1 tbl	Curry paste
1	Apple
2 stalks	Celery
	Sultanas
	Mayonnaise

METHOD

1. Chop the apple and celery into a fine dice.
2. Mix together the curry paste and mayonnaise.
3. Now mix together all the ingredients.

Cooks tip: Use only curry paste not curry powder, as curry powder is raw and needs to be cooked when used.

DELI SALAD
dressing

INGREDIENTS

2 tbl	Wine vinegar
Pinch	English mustard powder
6 tbl	Olive oil
2 tsp	Honey
2 tsp	Lemon juice

METHOD

1. Place all the ingredients into a screw top jar and shake well.

TABBOULEH
salad

6oz (180g)	Bulgar wheat
12 fl oz (360ml)	Boiling water
1 tsp	Salt
½	Cucumber, diced
1 bunch	Spring onions, diced
1lb (480g)	Tomatoes, chopped

DRESSING

3 fl oz (90ml)	Olive oil
3 fl oz (90ml)	Lemon juice
1 clove	Garlic, crushed
2 tbl	Fresh mint, chopped
4 tbl	Fresh parsley, chopped

METHOD

1. Mix the bulgar wheat with the salt, pour over the boiling water and leave for 15 minutes, until it absorbs all the water.
2. Mix all the ingredients together for the dressing and pour over the bulgar wheat and mix.
3. Leave for a few hours or overnight in a refrigerator.
4. Next day mix in the diced cucumber, spring onions and tomatoes.
5. Cover with dressing and serve.

Chicory
& orange salad

INGREDIENTS

4 bulbs	Chicory, chopped
3 sticks	Celery, sliced
½ bunch	Watercress
3	Medium oranges

DRESSING

3 fl oz (90ml)	Olive oil
2 fl oz (60ml)	Orange juice
¼ tsp	Dijon mustard
1 tbl	Parsley, chopped

METHOD

1. Mix together chicory, celery and watercress. Top with orange segments.
2. Combine dressing ingredients in a jar and shake well.
3. Sprinkle dressing over salad and serve.

COLESLAW

8oz (240g)	White cabbage
½	Onion, chopped
1	Carrot, grated
	Mayonnaise

METHOD

1. Trim off the outside leaves of the cabbage and cut into quarters, remove the centre stalk.
2. Shred finely.
3. Mix in the chopped onion and grated carrot.
4. Mix in the mayonnaise.

MAYONNAISE

INGREDIENTS

½ pt (300ml)	Olive oil
2	Egg yolks
2 tsp	Wine vinegar
½ tsp	English mustard
1 tsp	Lemon juice
1 tsp	Boiling water
	Salt and ground black pepper

METHOD

1. Place yolks, vinegar, mustard, lemon juice and seasoning in a bowl and whisk well.
2. Gradually pour in the oil very slowly, whisking continuously until mixture thickens.
3. Whisk in the boiling water.
4. Add seasoning to taste.

Desserts

CREME
b r u l e e

1pt (600ml)	Double cream
½	Vanilla pod
6	Egg yolks
1½ oz (45g)	Caster sugar
	Caster sugar for topping

METHOD

1. Gently heat the cream and vanilla pod in a saucepan.
2. Beat the egg yolks and sugar together and pour on the cream while continuing to beat.
3. Pour into six ramekins, place ramekins in a bain marie and place in a slow oven (300° F, 150° C, Gas mark 2) until just set.
4. Remove from oven and allow to cool completely.
5. Spread caster sugar on the top of each ramekin and place under a grill. Allow to brown gently.
6. Serve chilled with fresh grapes.

A THOLL
b r o s e

INGREDIENTS	
4oz (120g)	Rolled oats
¼ pt (150ml)	Whisky
2oz (60g)	Honey
½ pt (300ml)	Double cream

METHOD

1. Soak the oats in the whisky for approximately one hour, then stir in the honey.
2. Whisk the double cream and fold in oats.
3. Spoon into glasses, chill before serving.
4. Serve with fresh raspberries and shortbread.

Pink
grapefruit sorbet

4	Pink grapefruit
2oz (60g)	Sugar
1	Egg white
1	Lime

METHOD

1. Grate the skin of 1 grapefruit, then squeeze juice from the grapefruits and lime.
2. Make liquid up to ¾ pt (450ml) with orange or grapefruit juice if required.
3. Boil the sugar with ¼ pt (150ml) water and then add to fruit juice.
4. Place in freezer tray and freeze.
5. Whisk every 15 minutes.
6. Whisk egg white and add to sorbet as it begins to freeze to give sorbet smooth creamy texture.

LIME
s y l l a b u b

1pt (600ml)	Double cream
3	Fresh limes
3 fl oz (90ml)	Medium white wine
	Sugar to taste
	a little green vegetable colouring (optional)

METHOD

1. Grate the zest of two limes.
2. Squeeze the grated limes and place the juice with the zest into a bowl.
3. Add a little sugar and the white wine.
4. Leave to rest in a refrigerator for 1 hour (this will allow the flavours to permeate each other).
5. Whip the double cream and mix together with juice.
6. Pipe into chilled wine glasses.
7. Decorate with a slice of remaining lime and a sprig of fresh mint.
8. Serve chilled with a brandy snap biscuit.

CHOCOLATE
orange mousse

INGREDIENTS	
4oz (120g)	Plain chocolate
3	Eggs
1	Orange, for zest
1 tbl	Cointreau
1oz (30g)	Sugar
¼ pt (150ml)	Double cream or whipping cream

METHOD

1. Melt the chocolate in a basin over a saucepan of hot water.
2. Separate the yolks of eggs from the whites.
3. Mix the yolks with the chocolate and whisk together.
4. Add the zest of orange and Cointreau.
5. Whisk until frothy and keep warm.
6. Whisk the cream and keep to one side.
7. Whisk the egg white and sugar, keep to one side.
8. Fold the cream into the warm chocolate and then mix.
9. Now gently fold the egg white into the chocolate and cream mixture.
10. Spoon the mousse into individual glasses.
11. Decorate with whipped cream and chocolate curls.

SWEET PASTRY

5oz (150g)	Butter
2oz (60g)	Caster Sugar
1	Egg
8oz (240g)	Plain flour

METHOD

1. Cream together the butter and sugar.
2. Add the egg and thoroughly mix in.
3. Gradually mix in the flour until a smooth consistency is achieved.
4. Wrap the pastry in greaseproof paper and place in the fridge overnight before using.

ENID'S CHEESE

& apple pie

INGREDIENTS	
	Sweet pastry
1lb (480g)	Golden Delicious apples
6oz (180g)	Mature cheddar cheese
2oz (60g)	Sugar
	Ground cinnamon

METHOD

1. Line a 1pt (600ml) pie dish with half the pastry.
2. Peel and slice the apples.
3. Grate the cheese.
4. Layer apple slices and grated cheese until used up.
5. Sprinkle with sugar and ground cinnamon.
6. Roll out the remaining pastry and carefully lay the pastry over the dish.
7. Brush with milk and sprinkle with sugar.
8. Bake in a moderate oven (350° F, 180° C, Gas mark 4) for approximately 40 minutes.
9. Serve hot with either custard or fresh cream.

FRANGIPANE	
2oz (60g)	Butter
2oz (60g)	Caster Sugar
1	Egg
2oz (60g)	Ground almonds
1 dtsp	Plain flour
1 drop	Almond essence

METHOD

1. Cream butter and sugar, beat in egg. Mix in the almonds and flour. It is then ready to use.

Plum
p i t h i v i e r

8oz (240g)	Puff pastry
1 tbs	Plum jam
	Frangipane
8oz (240g)	Mirabelle plums
	Icing sugar

METHOD

1. Roll out ⅓rd of the puff pastry into a round 8 inch (20 cm), ¹⁄₁₆ inch (1mm) thick.
2. Moisten the edges and place on a greased baking sheet.
3. Spread the centre with the jam.
4. Slice the plums and place on jam.
5. Spread on the frangipane, leaving a 1 inch (2cm) border round the edge.
6. Roll out the remaining pastry, cut into a slightly larger round.
7. Place on top, seal and decorate edge.
8. Using a sharp pointed knife make approximately twelve curved cuts radiating from the centre to about 1 inch (2cm) from the edge.
9. Brush with beaten egg.
10. Bake in a hot oven (450°F, 230° C, Gas mark 6) for 25-30 minutes.
11. When cooked, sprinkle with icing sugar, return to a very hot oven to glaze (2-3 minutes).
12. Serve hot or cold.

Cakes
& bakes

Date
& walnut slice

6 fl oz (180 ml)	Evaporated milk
6oz (180g)	Chopped dates
4oz (120g)	Caster sugar
4oz (120g)	Butter
1 tsp	Vanilla essence
1	Egg, beaten
4oz (120g)	Self-raising flour
	Pinch of salt
3oz (90g)	Walnuts, chopped

METHOD

1. Bring the evaporated milk gently to simmering point.
2. Take off the heat and stir in the chopped dates.
3. Allow this mixture to cool.
4. Cream the butter with the sugar until light and fluffy.
5. Add the beaten egg and vanilla essence and mix in well.
6. Now fold in the sifted flour and salt together with the date mixture.
7. Stir in the chopped walnuts.
8. Place in a greased 9 inch (22cm) cake tin and bake (350° F, 180° C, Gas mark 4) for 30 - 35 minutes.
9. Turn out whilst warm and cut into slices.

Deli
f l a p   j a c k s

INGREDIENTS

4oz (120g)	Brown sugar
4oz (120g)	Butter
1 rounded dtsp	Golden syrup
6oz (180g)	Whole oats
½ tsp	Ground ginger

METHOD

1. First put the sugar, butter and golden syrup in a saucepan.
2. Heat gently until butter has melted, stirring occasionally.
3. Take off the heat and stir in the oats and ground ginger, mix thoroughly.
4. Now pour the mixture into a greased 8 inch (20cm) square baking tray and press it out evenly using a spoon.
5. Bake in the oven (300° F, 150° C , Gas mark 2) for 40 - 45 minutes.
6. Allow the flapjacks to cool in the tin for 10 minutes before cutting into oblong bars.
7. Leave until cold before removing.

SHORTBREAD
biscuits

INGREDIENTS	
3oz (90g)	Plain flour
3oz (90g)	Cornflour
4oz (120g)	Butter
2oz (60g)	Caster sugar
	Pinch of salt

METHOD

1. Sieve the plain flour, cornflour and salt.
2. Mix in the butter and sugar.
3. Mix all the ingredients to smooth paste.
4. Roll out on a floured board into a round shape ¼ inch (5mm) thick.
5. Place on a lightly oiled baking sheet.
6. Shape and prick with a fork.
7. Bake in a moderate oven (300° F, 150° C, Gas mark 2) for 15 - 20 minutes.

BRAN
t e a   b r e a d

3oz (90g)	All Bran
4oz (120g)	Sultanas
4oz (120g)	Mixed peel
8oz (240g)	Soft brown sugar
½ pt (300ml)	Milk
6oz (180g)	Self-raising flour
½ oz (15g)	Baking powder
	Pinch of nutmeg, cinnamon, mixed spice

METHOD

1. Mix the All Bran, fruit, sugar and milk in a bowl and leave to stand overnight, covered with a cloth.
2. Grease and line 9 inch x 5 inch (22cm x 12cm)loaf tin.
3. Sift flour, baking powder and spices into soaked ingredients.
4. Mix well and spoon into prepared tin.
5. Bake in the centre of oven (375° F, 190° C, Gas mark 5) for about 1¼ hours until well risen and just firm to touch.
6. Turn out, remove paper and cool on a rack.
7. Leave a day or two to mature, that is if you can wait that long!

BILLO'S
g i n g e r   c a k e

INGREDIENTS

8oz (240g)	Plain flour
4oz (120g)	Butter
2oz (60g)	Brown sugar
6oz (180g)	Golden syrup
2 tbl	Black treacle
2	Eggs, beaten
1 tsp	Mixed spice
2 tsp	Ground ginger
1 tsp	Bicarbonate of soda
4 fl oz (120ml)	Milk

METHOD

1   Sieve the flour, spices ginger and soda together.
2. Now place the sugar, butter, treacle and golden syrup into a saucepan.
3. Gently heat until the sugar, butter, treacle and syrup melt.
4. Allow to cool slightly before stirring the sieved dry ingredients into the mixture; also add the beaton eggs and milk. Thoroughly mix until smooth.
5. Pour into a pre-lined and greased 7 inch (17cm) square cake tin.
6. Place into a pre-heated oven (350°F, 150°C, Gas mark 2,) for approximately 1¼-1½ hours.
7. Test with a skewer. Cake is cooked when it comes out clean. Cool in tin before turning out.

CHOCOLATE
& hazelnut cookies

INGREDIENTS	
3oz (90g)	Unsalted butter
3oz (90g)	Caster sugar
2oz (60g)	Soft brown sugar
1	Egg, beaten
6oz (180g)	Self-raising flour
	Pinch of salt
2oz (60g)	Plain chocolate
1oz (30g)	Broken hazelnuts

METHOD

1. Cream together the butter, caster sugar and soft brown sugar.
2. Mix in the beaten egg, sieved flour and salt.
3. Stir in the chopped plain chocolate and broken hazelnuts.
4. Roll the dough into small balls and place onto oiled baking sheets.
5. Bake in a preheated oven (375° F, 190° C, Gas mark 5) for 12 - 15 minutes until golden brown.

Coconut
cupcakes

	INGREDIENTS
5oz (150g)	Butter
5oz (150g)	Caster sugar
2	Eggs, beaten
8oz (240g)	Plain flour
½ tsp	Baking powder
	Pinch of salt
2oz (60g)	Desiccated coconut
½ tsp	Vanilla essence
	Milk

METHOD

1. Cream the butter and sugar until soft.
2. Slowly add the beaten eggs, mixing continuously.
3. Gently mix in the sieved flour, baking powder and salt.
4. Add the desiccated coconut and vanilla essence.
5. The mixture should be a light dropping one. If necessary, add a few drops of milk.
6. Spoon into paper cake baking cases.
7. Bake in a hot oven (450° F, 230° C, Gas mark 6) for 15 - 20 minutes.